TARA TAKES FLIGHT

DEDICATION:

FOR MY SWEET PRINCESS:

SULTANA AKA SULLY

I WANTED TO MAKE A CHARACTER THAT WAS STRONG AND
CONFIDENT, A GIRL WHO NEVER GIVES UP AND TRIES HARD NO
MATTER WHAT TO ACHIEVE HER GOALS. THAT SWEET SMILE YOU
GIVE ME WHEN YOU ACCOMPLISH SOMETHING INSPIRED ME TO MAKE
TARA DACTYL A PERSON THAT ALL KIDS COULD LOOK UP TO.

DADDY LOVES YOU.

TARA DACTYL HAS A MOM AND DAD,
THEY'RE ALWAYS IN THE SKY
EVEN THOUGH SHE HAS A PAIR OF WINGS
SHE'S KIND OF SCARED TO FLY

DON'T KNOW WHY, MAKES HER CRY
AND SHE KNOWS SHE HAS TO TRY
BUT SHE'S NEVER BEEN THAT HIGH
MAYBE LESSONS SHE CAN BUY

IF HER FAMILY HELPS, SHE'S READY TO TRY IT
SHE CAN BE BRAVE
REMEMBERS THAT HER UNCLE TERRY'S THE FLYEST
IT'S HOW HE GETS PAID

HIS JOB IS TO BE AN INCREDIBLE PILOT,
GOT SKILLS FOR DAYS
HE SAID: "TARA I FIRST LEARNED HOW TO FLY WHEN I WAS YOUR AGE"

"IT'S OK, I CAN GIVE YOU COURAGE
THAT YOU NEED TODAY
DO YOUR THING YOU HAVE WINGS,
AND IT'S IN YOUR DNA"

"YOUR FAM WILL ALWAYS LOVE YOU
AND GIVE YOU A GREAT LIFE
SO CALL ME ANY TIME
YOU NEED PRACTICE TO TAKE FLIGHT"

SHE LOOKED UP TO THE CLOUDS
THOUGHT ABOUT IT AND SHE STARED
AND NOW SHE HAD THE CONFIDENCE
BECAUSE HER UNCLE CARED

PLUS, TERRY GAVE ADVICE
AND TARA WAS PREPARED
SHE FLEW UP IN THE AIR
AND WAS HAPPY SHE WASN'T SCARED

GRAFF SPOT

Freestyle Time: Color the pages how you want, add some cool graffiti, and write your own lyrics!!!

....

....

....

....

....

....

....

....

....

....

....

....

....

....

....

....

....

....

....

....

....

....

....

....

....

....

....

....

....

....

....

....

COVER AND BOOK DESIGN:
RENSFORD "REN" MONTROSE